SAND and MAN

by Willma Willis

with photographs collected by Lou Jacobs Jr.

AN ELK GROVE BOOK

CP   CHILDRENS PRESS, CHICAGO

For Inge
who always knows
where love lies
among the grains of sand

With special appreciation
to John Simpson.

Library of Congress Cataloging in Publication Data

Willis, Willma.
  Sand and man.

  SUMMARY: Describes the way sand is formed and
travels over the earth's surface and its many
uses to man.

  "An Elk Grove Book"

  1. Sand—Juvenile literature.   [1. Sand]
I. Jacobs, Lou, illus.   II. Title.
QE471.W525   553' .62   72-10184
ISBN 0-516-07619-1

1 2 3 4 5 6 7 8 9 10 11 12 13 14 15 16 17 18 19 20 21 22 23 24 25   R   75 74 73

Contents

Introduction

Everybody has seen *sand*. Buckets and shovels full of sand are spread in large boxes in the school yard. It fills your shoes when you climb sand hills, called *dunes*. Sand feels cool and hard on your bare feet when you race the waves at the beach. It is mixed with the dark soil in the flower bed and with the black oil that covers the street.

Sand shifts and rides on the swift desert winds, and it washes in streams and rivers and seas all over the earth. It piles up. It scatters far. Very, very slowly, the grains become smaller and smaller and finally wear away into dust. At the same time, grains by the millions are forming from larger pieces of rock.

Men have used the sand of beaches and rivers for centuries. From sandy shores they launch small boats and cast their fishing nets while their children dig holes in the sand.

We have found many other uses for sand. It serves us every day of our lives. You may not always recognize sand because it is often combined with other materials and looks quite different.

How is sand made? Where does it come from? How do we use it? What are the disguises it wears?

These are some of the questions we will explore in this book. Sand is really surprising!

1

Sand, the World Traveler

HOW SAND IS MADE

If you can find some, at home or in the school yard, or beside the road, pick up a handful of sand. Look at it closely. You can see it is made of tiny pieces of rock, all about the same size. Some grains are rounded and smooth. Most have sharp edges.

Long ago, before there was life on our earth, there was no sand. *Geologists* tell us the earth was first a mass of hot, molten rock. As it cooled and hardened, the surface rock wrinkled. It developed cracks and folds, but there was no sand or dirt or grass; no trees, insects, or animals of any kind.

Sand's life story began when this surface rock began to break up. It didn't break all by itself. Chemicals in the air and in the rock, along with moisture in the air, started the breaking-up process called *erosion*. Erosion goes on all over the earth, day and night, winter and summer, forever.

Rain and snow help erosion along when they freeze in the cracks of rocks. Ice is very strong, and it can pry great slabs off larger rocks and send them tumbling down the mountain. Pieces of all sizes break off as the rock tumbles down.

Perhaps you have seen a sign beside a mountain road that says, "Watch for falling rocks," or, "Slide area." Very often chunks of rock fall because ice has pried them

---

Rocks like these break up to become sand that mixes with soil, washes into rivers and often forms dunes in the desert.

off a larger rock.

When plants began to grow in the first crumbled rock at the beginning of time, acids, formed by living and dead plants, ate into the rocks. This helped to break them into smaller and smaller particles.

ROCKS INTO SAND

More than half of all the rocks on the earth's surface are two kinds, *feldspar* and *quartz*. Like all rocks, feldspar and quartz are composed of minerals, and most of the minerals are in the form of crystals.

Soon after feldspar breaks into fragments, these pieces crumble into powdery dust or clay.

Quartz is a very tough mineral. Its chief ingredient is *silicon*, the earth's most abundant material. Quartz crystals remain strong and hard and are found in many rocks. When rock, such as granite, containing quartz, breaks up and crumbles, the quartz crystals mingle with the *clays* and soils, but they do not wear away quickly. For this reason, quartz is the most important sand-making rock on the surface of the earth.

HOW SAND TRAVELS

We have talked about erosion, the process of wearing away the surface rocks, changing their shapes and moving them about.

Big rocks move very slowly, and sometimes not at all for hundreds or thousands of years. But, when the large rocks erode, and become sand, they really begin to travel.

Glaciers, streams, rivers, wind, and the ocean all

Quartz is a mineral made of silicon and oxygen and looks like glass. It is the most important sand-making mineral on earth.

carry on the work of erosion. All help break big rocks into little ones and move the pieces, sometimes to astonishing distances.

GLACIERS AND SAND

Glaciers are great masses of ice and snow. They lie across valleys in our highest mountain ranges and completely cover the Antarctic, except for the tips of the tallest mountain peaks.

Glaciers are sand makers. They move against the rock of the valleys and mountains beneath them, so slowly we cannot see the motion. As glaciers move they grind rocks against each other, breaking and smashing them into smaller fragments.

Glaciers are powerful erosion forces and sand makers, but they cover only a tiny part of the earth.

MOVING WATER AND SAND

Moving water does the most important work of erosion. In times of heavy rain and during the season when the warm sun melts the snow and ice, hundreds of streams form. They begin as tiny trickles, but these join to make larger streams, then rivers.

As the streams and rivers move down the slopes and through the hills and valleys, they, like the glaciers, pull and wash rocks from the earth. The water carries the fragments that break off: pebbles, gravel, sand, and mud.

Moving water also sorts its load of rock pieces. As it flows down and reaches flat land, it moves more slowly. The largest rock particles drop to the bottom or sides

---

Moving water carries sand and gravel that carves rocks, just as moving rivers carve deep canyons.

11

of the stream. But great amounts of sand, and the fine mud, called *silt*, continue to travel.

SAND AND THE SEA

Can you imagine yourself as a mile-tall giant taking a walk along the sea shores of every continent on earth? Look at a globe or a wall map, and you can see what a great journey that would be.

If you can pretend this kind of trip, you will see at nearly every stride an opening in the shoreline where the water from the land is flowing (or has flowed) into the sea.

Some of these openings are rivers several miles wide. Others are streams so small a boy of 10 could easily step across them.

Each one of these streams or rivers dumps sand and silt into the sea. Some of them pile up enormous banks of sand, silt, and mud, and these banks are called *deltas*. Large rivers like the Mississippi build deltas that extend for miles into the ocean in a fan-shaped pattern.

The great sweeping currents of the ocean capture the sand. Waves and tides act together to pull some of the sand deeper into the ocean and spread much of it along the shores. Sand dunes at the beach are built by the waves and tides and shaped by the wind.

Sometimes long strips of sand called *spits* or *hooks* or *sand bars* extend far out into the ocean, or build up in long narrow islands just off the shore. Like the deltas,

---

From 130 miles above the earth Apollo 9 Astronauts photographed the Colorado River where it drains into the Gulf of California (the dark area, lower right). Through the centuries the river brought sand and silt here and formed a delta. The light area at right is sand dunes.

these islands often support roads and buildings. Atlantic City, New Jersey, is a large city built on a sandbar.

When the rivers and streams of the world pour their water, sand, and silt into the sea, the stream water joins the ocean water, and a very special part of the sand story begins again.

The water evaporates from the surface of the sea. It rises into the atmosphere and makes clouds. The clouds travel over the land and drop rain and snow on the mountains and the hills and the valleys. Then the water begins its great journey again toward the sea, carrying another load of sand and silt. This cycle never stops. It has been going on since the earth first cooled and divided into seas and continents.

SAND IN THE DESERT

We have seen how glaciers and flowing water help to form sand and carry it to the ocean. Ice and water also help to form and carry the sands to some of the dry desert lands.

Even though water always flows toward the sea, sometimes it doesn't get there. Some streams are too small, and some come from springs that dry up during part of the year. Some streams carry water only when a sudden rainstorm fills them. Streams like these flow as long and as far as they can. Then they drop whatever sand and silt they carry and sink into the earth or dry up.

Now the wind, also very important in erosion, takes over. It lifts the smallest dry particles of dust and sand,

Sand builds bars and islands where rivers meet the sea. This picture shows Lynnhaven Bay (at left of photo) near Norfolk, Virginia. The dark water at the right is Chesapeake Bay.

15

swirling them into the air, sometimes in great clouds. When the wind stops blowing it drops the sand and dust it has been carrying, the heaviest first, the next heaviest next, and so on. The fine dust may be blown to another part of the country.

This leaves the sand behind. It accumulates in piles we call dunes. Desert sand dunes are piled and moved and constantly reshaped by the wind.

SANDSTORMS

When a strong wind blows and carries sand through the air, we call this a sandstorm. In the desert areas of the South Western United States, the wind may blow so much sand into the air that the sky is darkened. People in the area must drive their cars carefully. The wind-blown sand scars the paint and pits the windshields.

In desert lands all over the world the heavy particles of sand blown during sandstorms do the most work in shaping dunes. Sandstorms also "sandblast" surrounding rock faces, carving the surfaces into unusual shapes, pitting some, and polishing others.

Wind keeps changing the shape of dunes in Death Valley, California, and carves ripples in the sand.

2

Sand in Disguise

SEEING THROUGH SAND

What do you think of when you hear or see the word, "glass?" Probably you do not think of sand, but sand is the most important material in glass.

When you look through the window of your house or car, or when you look at an insect through a microscope at school, you are "seeing through sand." Almost all glass in everyday use is 60% to 80% sand.

As we learned in Part I, quartz is the most important sand-making mineral on earth. It is also the hardest of all common minerals. Actually, it looks like tiny pieces of broken or cracked glass.

Windows, microscope lenses, and drinking glasses are made by man, but nature was making glass for millions of years before man got the idea.

When lightning strikes quartz sand, the tremendous heat melts the sand grains so that they blend, or *fuse* together into long, slender tubes. These are called *fulgurites* or *"petrified lightning."*

When volcanoes erupt, they produce great heat which fuses sands into beautiful, smokey colored rocks called *obsidian* or *"volcanic glass."* For centuries Indians chipped obsidian into the arrow points they used to shoot game.

From volcanic rock called obsidian, the Indians made some of their arrow and spear points.

No one knows exactly when man first made glass. Probably he discovered it by accident. He may have built a very hot fire on a sandy spot and found afterward that the sand grains had melted together to make a hard, brittle material. Perhaps one time he poked in the fire with a stick and discovered that the melting, fused sand could be shaped before it cooled.

The first people to make glass for trade were the ancient Phoenicians. By about 1000 B.C. they were well-known for their glass containers of different shapes, sizes, and colors. They learned how to add other ingredients to the quartz sand to improve the strength and quality of their glass.

In most modern glass these other ingredients are *soda* (*sodium oxide*) and *lime*. When the quartz sand, soda, and lime are mixed together thoroughly and heated to a very high temperature, then cooled, the result is glass.

Man's skill and knowledge have made glass one of the most useful materials in the world. We continue to find new uses for it every year.

We could not have the electric light as we know it without the glass bulb. This glass is strong and thin enough to let the light through. Still it can be heated to a very high temperature without breaking or melting.

Glass can be shaped by blowing, rolling or molding. It is made into blocks that are used to make walls. It can be shaped into tubes larger than drinking straws and into ones so tiny they are like hairs or fibers.

Examples of ancient glass: on the left, a flask and in the center, a chalice, both from the Roman Empire, probably Syria, around the second or third century A.D. At right, a vase from Egypt made about 1350 B.C.

Glass fibers, or *fiberglass*, is extremely tough and lightweight. It can be woven, like yarn, into a kind of cloth often used for curtains. It is used to make the hulls of boats and the bodies of cars. It is formed into vaulting poles and fishing poles.

Recently a foam-type glass was developed that is so light in weight for the size of the piece that it floats.

Glass is one of the most surprising uses of sand, and one of its most common disguises.

SAND IN THE SIDEWALK

No matter where you live, in the city or the country, your hands or feet have touched sand today in another disguise.

Most schools and homes have sidewalks and driveways made of *concrete*. And sand is one of the most important ingredients in concrete. It is combined with gravel (like sand, but much bigger pieces), with water and *cement*, a material which is powdery when dry.

Cement is made from lime, *silica*, and *alumina*, materials that are mined from the earth. These materials are first crushed, then cooked in a huge oven. Then they are ground very fine, and another mined material, *gypsum*, is added at the last to control how fast the cement hardens.

When the sand and gravel and dry, powdery cement are mixed together with water, they make a thick, gray

Freeways and highways all over the world use many tons of sand in cement for the huge pillars and supports, and to form the smooth paving for roads.

mud—at first! As the mixture begins to dry, it gets thicker and thicker, and when it is completely dry, it is hard as rock.

Concrete is used in countless ways. Hundreds of thousands of miles of our finest highways are paved with concrete. Many homes, particularly in the West, have "concrete slab" floors. The concrete slab is covered by carpeting or plastic tiles to make it look pretty and keep it easy to care for.

Most tennis courts are giant-size concrete slabs, smoothed carefully so that the ball bounces where the player expects it to.

Foundations of buildings and bridges are made of concrete. The great dams that hold back the river water and store it for drinking and irrigation are made of concrete.

This hard, strong material is used to line huge ditches called *aqueducts* that carry water from the dams to the cities where it can be used.

SAND IN THE WALLS

If you want to fasten wooden blocks together in a tall tower so they won't fall, you may use glue to hold them together.

Mortar is a kind of "glue" that holds building bricks together, and mortar is made mostly of sand. The other main material in mortar is lime. Lime acts like cement when it is mixed with water and sand. The mixture is

This man puts a piece of colored glass into a wall held together by mortar made of sand and lime.

a thick, sandy liquid when the brick layer spreads it on the bricks. When dry, it becomes very hard and holds the bricks just as glue would hold pieces of wood together.

If the walls in your home or classroom are *plaster* walls, they too are made mostly of sand. Plaster is like mortar, but it's a smoother mixture with finer sand. It is mixed a little differently and is spread across the wall surface. Plaster can be painted any color, and it makes a very hard wall surface. When plaster is put on outside walls it is called *stucco*.

SAND IN THE STREET

The paved street where you ride your bicycle would not be so strong and long-lasting without sand.

The pavement is made of *asphalt*, a black, cement-like material found in *petroleum*, plus sand and gravel (or crushed rock).

Perhaps you have watched workers in your city pave a new street or patch an old one.

Big dump trucks bring loads of a black mixture of sand and asphalt from a nearby plant where it has been heated. Workmen spread it on the road, smoothing it carefully with big shovels and brushes. Then a man drives a heavy roller over the mixture to make it flat and hard.

Sand and lime are mixed in a turning barrel to make mortar that holds the bricks of the house together.

SAND IN THE GLASS IN THE STREET

Not long ago a group of engineering students at the University of Missouri decided to experiment with ways of using old bottles and jars that were thrown away.

Because glass is such a tough, long-wearing material, they thought it might be used in paving streets. They tried different mixtures, and found that the best one was about 60% crushed glass and 5% asphalt (like that used in other street paving) with stone dust and lime to hold it all together. They called their mixture *glasphalt*.

The first glasphalt used for street paving is on Raymer Avenue in Fullerton, California. The 600-foot section was completed while a crowd of school children and city officials watched.

The inventors of glasphalt say it should be helpful to drivers because the tiny bits of glass in the pavement reflect light and help them see better at night. Also, glass is so tough, it should make the pavement last longer.

SAND IN GLASS—IN WALLS AND FLOORS

The same company that first brought the glasphalt paving idea to Raymer Avenue continued to search for other good ways to recycle or re-use glass. They found that broken glass can be used in place of rock for making concrete building blocks.

In another experiment they used glass bits in place of marble chips or other stones to create beautiful *terrazzo* floors. These floors are made by mixing or pressing

Asphalt is dumped slowly from the truck and spread by the machine that follows, to pave this city street.

the glass pieces, marble, or pretty stones into wet cement, then polishing it smooth.

When you remember how glass and concrete are made, you know that the building blocks and the terrazzo floors make use of sand in two ways—in the glass and in the concrete.

SAND IN OUR WHEELS

Probably you would not put sand on the axle of your bicycle to make the wheel turn more easily. You know that oil, or another *lubricant*, is best for that job. Yet, surprising as it may seem, sand is an ingredient in a large family of man-made materials called *silicones*. In several of their many forms, silicones are very important lubricants.

Silicones are made of long-dead plants and animals combined with materials such as sand. Silicon, the basic material of silicones, is the most abundant material on earth, and the one that is the chief ingredient in quartz, the great sand-maker.

Different combinations of these materials make them into resins, paints, and varnishes for bridges and ships and to prevent rust. Silicone paints give the best protection for any structures that must last well in the rain, snow, ice, and wind.

You wouldn't put sand in a baking pan, but silicones are used in large bakeries to keep bread from sticking to the baking pans.

This picture was taken when Astronaut Neil Armstrong first stepped onto the hot surface of the moon. His boots had soles made of silicone rubber. Silicones, made partly of sand, resist heat, so these boots protected Armstrong's feet.

Silicones in electric motor parts make the motors last ten to 100 times longer than ever before.

Silicones are used in furniture polishes and in a special liquid that keeps your leather boots from soaking up water.

When you see your father rubbing the new car with silicone car polish, you will surely agree that silicones are a complete disguise for sand.

SANDSTONE

Sandstone is rock made up of millions of sand grains cemented together. The binding, or cementing material may be silica or clay or *carbonate of lime,* all present in nature. These cementing materials give the sandstone its color which ranges from white to dark gray or reddish brown.

Many buildings in the eastern part of the United States are made of sandstone. They are often called "brownstones."

The thick walls of this cathedral in Spain are made of sandstone, and the ancient window is stained glass, made mostly of sand.

3

Sand, the Tool

Man has developed many ways to use sand as a tool.

SANDPAPER

Sandpaper is made by gluing grains of sand, all the same size, to tough, heavy paper. It can be held in the hand or attached to a mechanical sander. You can buy sandpaper that is very coarse to extra fine and use it to smooth the surfaces of wood to make them ready for paint or varnish.

Circles of sandpaper, *sanding discs*, can be fastened to a motor and turned very rapidly. A furniture maker uses sanding discs to smooth the legs for a table. *Sanding belts* driven by motors are used to sand large areas such as wooden floors.

Sandpaper is an *abrasive.* This name is used for any substance that grinds, smooths, sharpens, and polishes various materials. Other abrasives are made by compressing sand grains together into the shape of a thick stone-like wheel that is turned by a motor. This is a *grinding wheel.* It is hard and tough enough to smooth hard metal and sharpen knives and other tools.

Carborundum is another abrasive. It is made of sand and carbon. It is one of the most important abrasives and is used to cut and grind very hard metals.

A grinding wheel throws sparks as it cuts metal.

Perhaps your father has a small, flat block he calls a "sharpening stone" or "whetstone." He sharpens kitchen knives and other metal tools with it. First he dips the stone in water, then he rubs the knife edge on the surface of the stone. This "stone" is made of carborundum.

SANDBLASTING

Another use of sand as a tool is *sandblasting*.

Sand, forced under high pressure through a hose or pipe, will cut the surface it strikes. This is called sandblasting. Sandblasting will take old paint off large buildings or clean dirt and grease off stone-surfaced buildings. It will remove rust or scale from ships or bridges to prepare them for fresh paint.

Sandblasting is also a way of making glass *translucent*. The sand cuts tiny nicks in the glass and changes the way the light goes through. Light will pass through translucent glass, but you cannot see clearly through it. Sometimes bathroom windows are made this way.

SAND BAGS

On stormy days when big waves crash against the shore, home owners may call for sand bag help. Sand bags are large cloth, burlap, or plastic sacks filled with sand and piled up to form temporary dams. The dams help keep waves from cutting at the foundations of buildings. Oceanfront home owners often store a supply

Sand mixed with water is shot from a hose to sandblast old paint from this wall before it is repainted.

of empty sacks which they can fill quickly with beach sand when they need them.

FILTERING

Nobody wants sand in his drinking water, and something is wrong with the system if you find it in yours. However, in many of our cities sand is very important in making the water clear so that you like the way it looks and tastes.

The water supply for most cities is brought from rivers or storage reservoirs. It must be cleaned before it is pure enough for people to drink and use in their homes.

First the water flows to a treatment plant where chemicals are put into it. These chemicals gather bacteria and dirt into little blobs that sink to the bottom.

Next, the filtering begins. A *filter* is any kind of a screen that lets air or light or liquid through while preventing other materials from passing through.

Sand is a very good filter for water. The water flows over a bed of clean sand several feet deep and slowly sinks through the sand to a lower level. The sand collects particles and impurities still left in the water after the first treatment.

Finally, after the water filters through the sand, it goes on to another reservoir for treatment to destroy any remaining bacteria.

Bags of sand are used to build a temporary dam or to keep water from overflowing banks.

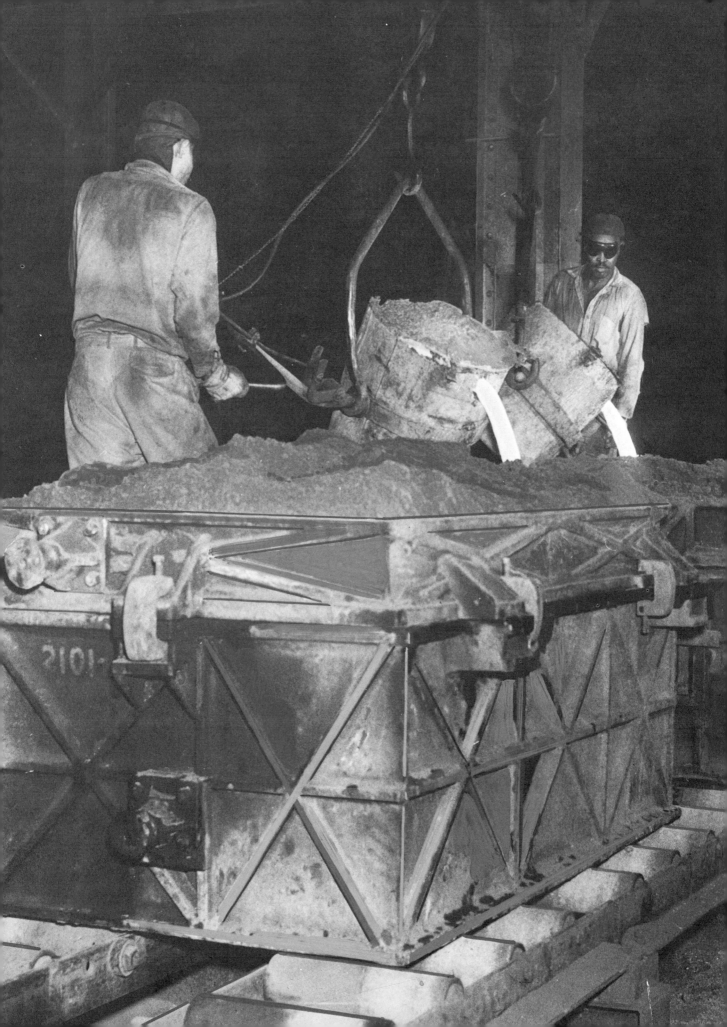

SAND CASTING

Perhaps you have seen a big brass bell in a park or museum or church steeple. No bell is made of sand, and it is not sandy when you see it, but it was made with a great amount of help from sand. The bell is shaped by pouring hot metal into a mold made of sand.

First, a pattern is carved, often of wood, in the exact shape the bell is to be. Sand is packed around the pattern, then the pattern is carefully removed so that the sand remains in the shape of the pattern. Next the hot metal is poured into the mold.

When the metal cools it can be lifted out of the sand. The sand is brushed off, and the metal has the shape of the pattern. This is called a *sand casting*.

Metal, to be poured, must be extremely hot. If poured into a wooden pattern, the molten metal will burn the wood and spoil the shape. However, the metal is not hot enough to melt the sand. When cool, a sand casting stays in the shape of the pattern.

Anchors of large ships are usually cast in a sand mold. The part of the automobile that holds the pistons and other moving parts, the engine block, is a sand casting.

The place where sand castings are made is called a *foundry*.

You can make a sand casting if you can find very fine-grained wet sand and some old candles to melt. Ask your mother to show you how to melt the wax safely. Perhaps she will lend you a shallow ash tray for a pattern. Press your pattern into the wet sand, upside down.

These men pour molten iron into sand molds to make cast iron shapes.

41

Push it hard so that sand comes up into the cupped part of the pattern. Then remove the pattern carefully. Slowly pour liquid wax into the sand mold. It will cool and harden into the shape of the tray you used for a pattern.

SAND ON THE TRACKS

Sand boxes can be tools. They are different from the sand box you used to play in.

Near the wheels of a railroad train's locomotive are sand boxes controlled by the engineer in the cab. These drop sand on the tracks to keep the wheels of the locomotive from slipping when it climbs a steep grade or starts off with an extra heavy load.

Along many highways in cold climates sand boxes stand beside the road near the base of a hill. A driver can spread some of the sand on the icy road. The sand makes a rougher surface so the tires won't skid and slide.

A much larger "sand box" is more like a tank full of sand, mounted on a truck. This is a *sand spreader*. It sprinkles a mixture of sand and salt, or sometimes sand alone, on icy streets. The salt melts the ice, and the sand keeps the tires from slipping.

Sand on the track and the roadway helps us arrive alive!

These locomotive wheels and other parts were cast in sand molds, then polished with abrasives containing sand.

4

Discovering Beaches and Dunes

Perhaps the place you think of first when you see the word, "sand," is a favorite beach, or the shore of a lake or large river.

Most of these sands are made of the mineral, quartz. But there are other sands, too, of unusual materials and surprising colors.

BLACK SANDS OF KALAPANA

A boy who lives on the island of Hawaii near Kalapana Beach may think of the color black when he thinks of sand. Along this beach the black sand is tiny grains of *lava*.

The lava which formed this black beach flowed down the slopes of a great volcanic mountain. When the hot, molten mass hit the cool water, it cooled so rapidly that it shattered into pieces.

Centuries of washing and wearing by the waves smoothed and rounded the lava fragments into the sand of Kalapana Black Sand Beach. Lava sand feels rough under bare feet because the particles are larger than the sand grains on most other beaches.

GREEN AND WHITE BEACHES

Also on the island of Hawaii is a green lava beach. The sands here were made by a kind of lava that contains the green mineral, *olivine*.

On the island of Hawaii, Kalapana Beach is an unusual black sand that is actually tiny grains of lava.

On other shores of the Hawaiian Islands are beaches of fine-grained white sand. The rock that forms these beaches is made of plants, long dead, and sea animals, such as shellfish and *coral*. Coral is a stony material that is formed by colonies of tiny sea creatures called *polyps*. Much of the land of the Hawaiian Islands is coral which has accumulated for millions of years under the sea. Great earth movements raised the coral-covered ocean floor above the sea to become islands.

Then, as the ocean pounded and pounded upon the shores, the coral broke into smaller and smaller bits. Finally it became the sandy white beaches that are the most beautiful and best places in Hawaii for swimming and surfing.

OTHER SANDY SHORES

Most lakes have at least one sandy shore. Usually this is near the main inlet, the point where a large stream or river flows into the lake.

Along the eastern shore of the great Lake Michigan are sand dunes that rise as high as 600 feet, and people enjoy a wonderful sport—riding over them in dune buggies. Dune buggies, sometimes called dunesmobiles, are automobiles fitted with extra large tires. The tires do not get stuck in the sand, and the driver can take his buggy up and down, over and around, anywhere he wants to drive, without having to follow a road.

DESERT SANDS—THINK WHITE, PINK, OR TALL

If you live far from lakes or great rivers or oceans, you may think first of the sand you see in desert dunes.

Streams and rivers carry sand to the sea where ocean waves shape it into beaches.

In the desert land of New Mexico, are dunes so daz- zling white that you must shade your eyes to look at them in the sunlight. These dunes are made entirely of gypsum, a mineral that has washed out of the rock in the surrounding desert mountains, and also from the floor of the basin. For thousands of years this material has piled up in dunes. As white and fine-grained as sugar, it has been carved and moved by desert winds.

These dunes are named White Sands National Mon- ument. Every year thousands of people visit here to play and picnic. Some even bring their skis and practice skiing on the slopes of the white gypsum sand.

If you have ever been in Southern Utah, you may think of the color pink when you think of sand. Near Zion and Bryce National Parks are hundreds of square miles where the earth is covered with a layer of pink sand. In some places it is as bright as the inside of a watermelon.

Much of the rock in the bluffs and mountains of this country is red sandstone. As we learned in Part I, water and weather erode and crumble the rock. It washes down the slopes to become the sand that is picked up and ground even finer by the wind. Everything except the green trees and shrubs and flowers in this beautiful land seems to be colored pink or red.

On the Coral Pink Sand Dunes near Kanab, Utah, you may even see pink grasshoppers. They are so per- fectly matched to the pink sand that they are invisible until they jump!

Some of the biggest dunes in the United States are

At White Sands National Monument the dunes are gypsum, which is whiter and finer-grained than most beach sands.

in the state of Colorado. A few are 500 to 700 feet high, or as tall as a 25-story building. They are composed of rock eroded to fine particles from the mountains that surround this great desert bowl. The mountains are capped with snow for much of the year, so you know that glaciers crushed the rock and rushing water helped grind it fine and bring it down to the desert floor. This is the Great Dunes National Momument.

SINGING SANDS OF THE EMPTY QUARTER

Besides these great sandy areas in the United States, there are others in the world much larger. In the Southeast corner of Saudi Arabia is a sand-covered land about the size of our state of Texas. It is called the Empty Quarter because no people live there.

American companies have found oil under this desert. The engineers and workers who direct and operate the oil wells must fly back and forth to visit the wells. All of the heavy oil-drilling equipment, however, has to travel across the dunes on big trucks with special tires, somewhat like the dune buggy tires. The driver finds his direction with a compass because the shifting sands cover a road track in a very short time.

These sands are sometimes called the "singing sands." The "song" is heard when you walk on a dune near its crest and cause the sand to slip. The layers of sand make the sound as they shift and rub against each other under your weight.

An oil company sand buggy carries workers and equipment across Saudi Arabia's Empty Quarter, a vast area of dunes almost the size of Texas.

5

So What Else Is Sandy?

SAND FOR SALE

After kindergarten or first grade, most boys and girls don't care very much about playing in sand boxes, but these are important play spots in city parks and school yards. Young people who live far from the beach or desert or sandy shore of a lake or river get their first idea of sand from sand boxes.

Usually a sand and gravel company brings the sand to the parks and schools. This company digs the sand from the earth or from a dry river bed and separates it into particles of different sizes for different uses. Sometimes a sand and gravel company will crush larger pieces of rocks into man-made sand of the sizes needed.

The sand and gravel company sells sand to the city's street paving department and to the construction company that makes the concrete sidewalks. It sells sand to companies that build the concrete foundations for houses and schools and industrial plants. And it sells sand to the *contractors* who plaster the walls of all of these buildings.

This kind of company fills the bags used to build temporary dams that keep a river from overflowing its banks.

The machines in a sand and gravel plant screen the sand before it is used for making concrete and paving streets.

SAND PAINTINGS

Since there are sands of different colors, it's not too surprising that men have used colored sand in their art.

The Navaho Indians of the Southwestern United States are noted for their sand paintings. They make this sand by grinding up colored rocks from the surrounding countryside.

The sand paintings are important in ceremonies, especially the Medicine Man's healing rites. He selects colors from tiny sand piles beside him and drizzles the sand through his hand in a fine stream to form beautiful designs. No two sand paintings are ever the same. The Medicine Man destroys his sand paintings as soon as he finishes his ceremony.

THE HOURGLASS

Would you believe that sand was very important for centuries in helping men measure time? It was put into a device called an *hourglass*.

This is two bulbs of glass, joined by a small opening. One bulb is filled with fine, dry sand. Exactly one hour is required for the sand to flow through the narrow opening into the bulb below.

Half-hour glasses, and even minute glasses were used before men had mechanical clocks. These sand timepieces were very accurate because the sand flows at an even rate of speed, no matter how much of it is in the glass.

Perhaps you have an egg timer in your home. This

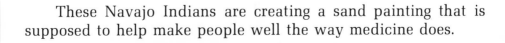

These Navajo Indians are creating a sand painting that is supposed to help make people well the way medicine does.

is built like an hourglass, but it is made so that the sand flows from one bulb to the other in about three minutes, the length of time it takes to soft-boil an egg.

QUICKSAND

If you removed a bucket of quicksand from its pit, it would look much like any other sand, except that it is very, very fine-grained. When dry, it looks almost like powder.

Quicksand is very deep and is usually found in the bottoms of streams and on sand flats along the seacoast.

When water is forced upward through this sand, the grains push apart, losing their firmness so that they cannot support weight. Many people have lost their lives in quicksand. They did not realize that what looked like wet sand was really deep, watery sand with no solid earth beneath.

If you ever find you have made such a mistake, don't struggle. Lie flat on your back with your arms out at the sides, and you will float on the quicksand. Then, slowly roll toward firm ground.

A good way to test, if you suspect you are looking at quicksand, is to throw a large object into it. If the object sinks, don't go after it. Stay clear!

In early times people used the hourglass as a clock. The sand flows from top to bottom at the same speed every time.

57

SANDMAN

If you have been interested to read this much about sand, you may feel, as we do, that discussing the Sandman is the right way to end our story of sand and all of its surprises.

The Sandman is a legendary figure who comes at night to put children to sleep by closing their eyes with sand. If you can remember feeling very sleepy and trying to keep your eyes open, you know that your eyes feel as though there are little grains under the lids.

Some mother or father or other story-teller, centuries ago, probably invented the Sandman to explain to a child why his eyes felt sandy when he was about to go to sleep.

These sand paintings and sculpture were part of an art museum show in Glendale, California. People walked on paths between them.

Glossary / Index

60

Picture Credits

Corning Glass Works, p. 8, 18, 20

National Aeronautics and Space Administration, p. 12, 30

Environmental Protection Agency, U.S. Dept. of Interior, p. 14

Division of Highways, State of Calif., p. 22

Borg-Warner Plumbing Products, p. 40

Hawaii Visitors Bureau Photo, p. 44

Washington State Dept. of Commerce and Economic Development, p. 46

Kodak, p. 48

Arabian American Oil Co., p. 50

Bureau of Indian Affairs, p. 54

The Corning Museum of Glass, p. 8, 18, 20

General Electric Co., p. 30